Going For Impact
The Nonprofit
Director's Essential
Guidebook

GOING FOR IMPACT
THE NONPROFIT
DIRECTOR'S ESSENTIAL
GUIDEBOOK

What to Know, Do and Not Do

based on a veteran director's
ample field experience

Eugene H. Fram with Vicki Brown

ISBN: 1530496349
ISBN 13: 9781530496341
Library of Congress Control Number: 2016904447
CreateSpace Independent Publishing Platform
North Charleston, South Carolina

CONTENTS

INTRODUCTION

Do you know what's expected of you if you are a new director on a nonprofit board? Already on a board and asking, "Are we making a difference?" Questioning if what you know about directors' fiduciary and legal responsibilities is up to date? Orienting new board members? Planning the board retreat? Wondering about the lack of fundraising efforts?

Or are you serving on a board developing a strategic plan? Struggling to develop data and information that really show what the nonprofit achieves? Searching for a new CEO or executive director? Considering potential merger?

If these or a host of other related questions describe you or your board, this guidebook is for you.

You Will Learn

- What your fiduciary and legal responsibilities are.
- Where the boundary line is between your director responsibilities and that of management, so you avoid "micromanaging" staff.
- What it takes for your board to set real strategic goals and measure progress toward them in meaningful ways.
- The essential ways nonprofit boards differ from their for-profit counterparts.
- How to do succession planning long before there's ever a need for a new CEO or executive director.
- That your board has a responsibility to *overview* the staff talent bank in order to be able to identify future leaders.
- There are critical steps to take to onboard and support a new top leader.
- What's needed for the board to develop a strategic plan in partnership with management.
- How to ensure the strategic plan isn't something the board and management put on a shelf but instead keep at center stage.
- What issues to address if exploring merger with another nonprofit.
- And much more!

But Why this Particular Guidebook?

It's practical, up-to-date, clear (and thanks to my writer/ editor, also engaging!) and most of all, useful – now and long into the future.

Start with the realization that for a nonprofit in the U.S. an organization's mission is commonly framed in terms of impact. That would seem to make the role of the nonprofit board member easy to describe. *The job of the volunteer director is to help the nonprofit hit the mark in delivering impact.*

The problem is this description makes the job sound like one with clear direction. Unfortunately that doesn't reflect what's happening in the real world. Far too often nonprofit board members are left to figure out on their own exactly what they need to know, what actions they should take and which pitfalls to sidestep as they seek to move their own nonprofit forward. Responsibilities that should be but aren't fulfilled by the board usually fall by default to the CEO or executive director. Deep experience in the nonprofit arena has taught me that's not a happy outcome for either the board or top executive.

The catalyst for writing *Going for Impact: The Nonprofit Director's Essential Guidebook* is my service on 12 very different nonprofit boards and five diverse for-profit ones over more than 30 years' time, plus my work as a nonprofit and business consultant across the U.S. Helping nonprofit board members do their jobs more effectively is my passion because it's critically important work.

According to the Urban Institute, there are about 1.41 million registered nonprofits in the nation. (That doesn't count religious congregations or organizations with less than $50,000 in annual revenues because they don't have to register.) Approximately 35% of registered nonprofits were required to file Form 990 (or 990-EZ or 990-PF) with the IRS in 2013. This group alone reported revenues of $2.26 trillion and expenses of $2.10 trillion, and were managing assets valued at $5.17 trillion.[1]

How did I approach writing this guidebook? The answer is from your perspective. Consider Section One. Titled "Essentials to Know," it proceeds to address six key areas in a straightforward, concise way. For example, the elephant in the boardroom may be too much deference to other directors or the board chair. Another topic is about what a board should expect from management, starting with "no surprises or spin." You'll also find brief examples or stories from the real (not some theoretical) world woven throughout the guidebook. They are used to explain or underscore points that are important to know.

A glance through the easy-to-use index at the end of this guidebook, and a quick look at the table of contents, will show you it's not designed for just one-time use. It's also been crafted with your future needs in mind. *Going for Impact* is a resource you can reach for (or keep on your digital device) when you need guidance at any time — whether you are on your current board or on any others that you step up to serve.

This guidebook will save you time and energy, and most importantly, enable you to utilize your talents more quickly and effectively on behalf of the community, clients, members or others you are legally obligated to represent as board director.

Anyone who's ever served on a dysfunctional board knows it's exhausting, frustrating and amazingly time-consuming. But there's one thing I've learned for certain about being a nonprofit director that I want to emphasize. Serving on a high performance nonprofit board that works appropriately in partnership with management to make a difference is one of life's extremely rewarding experiences. *Going for Impact* can help you and your board get there!

Eugene H. Fram, Ed.D.

Acknowledgments

I f you are involved in the nonprofit sector, either as volunteer or paid staff, you are making an incredible difference in our country. On behalf of the clients and institutions you work so hard to serve, thank you for your countless contributions. From my vantage point, figuratively speaking, you stand 10 feet tall.

I add a heartfelt personal thank you to the colleagues, friends and others in the nonprofit sector that I've worked with or learned from over the years. You inspire my work and I'm grateful.

ESSENTIALS TO KNOW

CHAPTER 1

BE AWARE OF ROSE-COLORED GLASSES

B
eing asked to join a nonprofit board is, in itself, an honor. Working alongside other directors for a cause that addresses world, community, professional or association needs commonly evokes a mix of pride, loyalty and reverence. Call it the nonprofit "mystique." Be aware, though, that you risk becoming an honorary placeholder on your nonprofit board if you hang on to rose-colored glasses. To recognize common "mistakes" that can keep you and your board colleagues from being truly effective, you must see clearly what's real and what's not. When you hear any of these commonly voiced assertions, look beyond surface realities.

- *Our board is doing a great job!*
    Ask yourself, "What does that mean?" Does board goal setting and verification of impacts and compliance policies reflect only satisfaction with the status quo? Or is the board setting stretch

goals and motivating management and staff to maximize client service?

- *We have no worries – we have (or just hired) a great CEO (or Executive Director)!*
  Monitoring this critical position isn't about checking off any of the following:
  o He/she is "minding the store."
  o There's been modest, incremental growth.
  o Our board chair reports the CEO is great.
  o The board "check box" survey shows no concerns with our top leader.
  Monitoring the top leader actually involves a robust evaluation that's conducted annually.

- *When push comes to shove, our board can raise big $$!*
  Recognize that recent national statistics show the opposite. Nearly two-thirds of nonprofit CEOs gave their boards academic grades of "C" or below for their fundraising efforts — and this in an age of rampant grade inflation![2] Don't abdicate fundraising responsibility to the CEO or, at times, ignore his or her pleas for help. Instead, fully partner with your CEO to develop resources for the organization.

- *Our programs are superior to other similar nonprofits!*
  Making a point-by-point comparison is something an alert board should do every three years.

"Comparison shopping" provides a clear picture of your organization's strengths and weaknesses and, in the event of under performance, will be the catalyst for relevant discussion on what to do about any gap(s).

- *Our board of directors is like a family!*
  Remind yourself that families don't typically meet once a month, serve specific terms, or weigh whether to resign when faced with overwhelming work/personal pressures. A nonprofit board is not a family and shouldn't aspire to be one.

Takeaway

It is entirely appropriate for a director to act as cheerleader for the nonprofit and, in fact, that's what directors are supposed to do. But first remove the tinted glasses and take a hard look at what's happening inside, then enlist your colleagues in an effort to right the ship or seize the potential for improving client services. That's when you will have compelling reason to spread the word!

CHAPTER 2

BE WARY OF A "SILENT" BOARDROOM

On far too many nonprofit boards, the amount of discussion and the expression of differences of opinion by board members — regardless of the issue at hand — is modest, at best. Almost always the elephant in the room is too much deference by directors toward others on the board. Thoughtful, experienced nonprofit directors will be familiar with the following two scenarios.

A) **Too much deference by directors toward fellow board members**

This type of deference is probably due, in large part, to the fact that nonprofit directors typically don't have much financial risk and only a low chance of reputational risk. In addition, while directors' dedication to the mission of the nonprofit will range from limited to fervent, there is no compelling reason for directors to make strong statements or to openly convert others to their viewpoints.

Plus many directors may want, for reasons unrelated to the nonprofit, to have future contacts with directors who have a different opinion regarding the issue at hand. In other words, people don't want to jeopardize their interpersonal relationships with other directors or their networks. Realize, for example, that it's quite common for a major donor on a nonprofit board to receive a great deal of deference. After all, who wants to be responsible for openly challenging the donor, especially one who might abruptly resign, with the challenger then incurring the wrath of the entire board?

When this scene plays out board meeting after board meeting there seems to be little potential for "healthy conflict" among the directors themselves, unless the very survival of the organization is in question. That's why the strongest stand that most directors take in this type of scenario is to vote "no" on an important issue and then quietly resign, using the usual excuse of increased job pressures.

B) Too much deference to the board chair

In this scenario board chairs receive excessive deference in decision-making. While such board chairs (like all board chairs!) can use *Robert's Rules of Order* as the basis for managing conflicts, few do. An example of a clear deviation from accepted procedures is for a board chair to simply make a "T" hand signal to signal a break in discussion — and receive no protest from other directors! Another giveaway that there's excessive deference is when someone in a leadership role (typically CEO or board chair) boasts that the non-profit board operates only on a consensus basis.

Yet the most common demonstration of excessive deference is when directors simply acquiesce to the board chair's viewpoint because they see it as a courtesy to a fellow volunteer who wants to move the meeting along with alacrity. Directors in this scenario don't engage in critical thinking when they should, and often fail to recognize the resulting impact can be serious, potentially up to and including personal financial fines for the inadequate discharge of their legal "due care" board responsibilities.

Takeaway

Never underestimate the limiting power of a nonprofit board's culture. Directors who want to serve on high performance boards need to stay alert to the deference directors give one another and especially the board chair during meetings. Too much deference, as will be noted in a later chapter, is particularly a problem during substantive discussions of policy and strategy.

Note: For simplicity's sake, the term CEO, when it appears on subsequent pages of this guidebook, should be assumed to reference not only the chief executive officer but also other common titles used by nonprofits for the top paid leader (e.g., executive director, executive secretary, president).

CHAPTER 3

WHAT MAKES A NONPROFIT BOARD GREAT

I t is a common misconception that you measure how "great" a nonprofit board is by the number of people on it who have exceptional qualifications, notably prominence in the community, achievements in business or civic roles, or highly regarded professional degree(s). Yet experience teaches the engaged director the far more meaningful gauge is the way board members work together.

Many descriptors can be applied to a great board, but there are three that are hallmarks: a) the quality of boardroom dialogue and debate is high; b) the board demonstrates it can ask tough questions of management; and c) directors are diverse in both experience and thought.

Each of the above carries its own hidden challenge but also a solution that's frequently overlooked by board members.

The quality of boardroom dialogue and debate is high

Challenge: Even on boards that meet monthly for a couple of hours, directors don't have enough interactive time to get to know one another. In addition, most board members, as noted earlier, tend to avoid conflict because it can easily lead to interpersonal problems.

Solution: The board chair and CEO need to develop a board culture that allows for vigorous dissent as a positive process. The board chair, in particular, needs to be aware if deference is shown to him/her, the CEO or other directors. The chair has many options, including posing potential "conflicts" about solutions for issues, which can be a big catalyst for improving the quality of a board discussion.

The board demonstrates it can ask tough questions of management

Challenge: As volunteers, nonprofit directors often make decisions about issues that are far afield from their career experience or personal interests.

Solution: Directors need to take time to better understand the environment in which the nonprofit operates. Yet even when a director doesn't have extensive background with an area (or issue) under discussion, it is possible to raise fair and rigorous questions (e.g., level of due diligence behind a recommendation, impact of the proposal on future budgets). Even if there is a risk of embarrassing management or initiating conflict on the board, a director is duty bound to ask these types of questions.

If a board member's questioning becomes a harangue or obstructs reasonable progress, the board chair needs to offer "constructive feedback" to the individual on the quality of his or her contributions. Feedback also should be given privately to directors at the other end of the scale – that is, those who routinely avoid questioning management.

Directors are diverse in both experience and thought

Challenge: Most nonprofit boards select members on the basis of professional experience (e.g., marketing, accounting, human relations) and demographic considerations. But such selection does not ensure that the board has members who have capabilities critical to the nonprofit's future. The single most important one is strategic perspective – and every nonprofit needs some members with it.

Solution: Finding candidates with capabilities that are critical to a specific board can only be done by reputation, not by career background. Developing such a board, within the confines of maximum board membership, is necessary to achieve diversity of thought. This requires creative recruiting because such recruits are not typically the friends, family and colleagues who now populate the majority of nonprofit recruitment pools. Board candidates who are recruited need to understand director responsibilities or be willing to learn about them on the job.

Takeaway

Rarely do nonprofit directors vote "no" to record a different perspective on a proposal. Rigorous but fair questioning of management must be the norm rather than what is far too often the case today with directors voting "yes" either to go along or to avoid conflict.

The need for diversity on nonprofit boards has been well documented for decades, but a new view is evolving that calls for nonprofits to develop inclusive boards. Being inclusive is not just about demographic considerations. The term also needs to encompass differences in experience, thought and stakeholder perspective. In fact, some boards have moved in the direction, where legal by state law, to have the CEO as an ex-officio member or voting member of the board to represent staff stakeholders.

CHAPTER 4

The responsibilities of nonprofit directors fall into two categories. They either mirror the responsibilities of directors in the for-profit world or they are specific to the nonprofit based on its bylaws and culture. The former are well understood and drive board action. The latter are what can make nonprofit directors' duties more difficult than those of their for-profit counterparts. Nonprofit-only responsibilities, however, are not fully addressed in the nonprofit world. Many are, in fact, "latent duties" because they are so often dormant or invisible.

- *The five duties that are the same for directors on nonprofit and for-profit boards*
  a) Fiduciary responsibilities — in general they include not profiting from one's relationship

with the organization and avoiding conflicts of interest

b) Establishing, with staff input, the organization's mission, vision and values

c) Setting policies and strategies

d) Overviewing outcomes and their impacts

e) Conducting annual meetings

- *There are other duties that apply specifically to nonprofit directors*

 Fundraising: Whether or not a nonprofit's bylaws list fundraising as a board responsibility, actually raising funds is too often left to the CEO and/or a development director. In a recent survey, 76% of 1,340 nonprofit CEOs gave their boards academic grades of C, D or F for their fundraising efforts.[3] Fundraising is most effective when there is an active partnership between the board and the CEO.

 Legal Requirements: Nonprofit directors have legal requirements that aren't incumbent on for-profit directors.

 ○ IRS 990 Form: A nonprofit board is required to participate in development or review of the IRS 990 Form in detail before it is submitted each year. Nonprofit directors must adhere to the regulations established by the state in which the nonprofit is located. In California, for example, "…a charity may sometimes be required to file a 990 with the state's attorney general, even when there is no requirement that a 990 be filed with the IRS."[4]

○ <u>IRS Intermediate Sanctions Act:</u> Very few nonprofit directors and managers are aware of this Act, which is related to excess benefits transactions (Section 4958 of the IRS Code). If directors or managers provide an excess benefit to themselves, an employee or even a volunteer, they can incur serious personal tax penalties. Examples of excess benefits might include such things as providing above market salaries or selling something to a volunteer at below market value.

○ <u>Knowing Who the Board Represents:</u> Nonprofit boards legally represent a community, professional organization or trade association. For example, a local charity board represents the interests of the community while a professional board represents the interests of the group's members. A nonprofit's legal standing is what allows it to function with tax-free status and acquire other benefits. Nonprofit directors sometimes mistakenly assume their jobs are to represent the interests of staff as well as (or instead of) the groups they legally represent. This is a perceived responsibility that doesn't exist.

Building Board-Staff Trust: Developing a relationship with the nonprofit's staff is typically an unstated, yet critical duty of a nonprofit board so that the board understands the environment in which the nonprofit operates. In addition, most nonprofit organizations are relatively flat organizations with staff only one or two levels below the board on the organizational chart. As a result, staff members are well attuned to the actions of their boards and know that directors, unlike those on for-profit boards, rotate frequently, potentially opening the door for influential directors who want to make rapid, emotionally charged changes. For example:

> *Two new board members succeed in initiating a board-mandated, yet bureaucratic Management by Objectives Program into a nonprofit's operations. This results in staff spending hours completing and reviewing MBO forms, which reduces productivity and lowers morale.*

Board directors need to seek greater contact with staff (e.g., at staff celebrations of success, via board-staff committees, at other appropriate occasions). This builds trust, which is essential. At the same time, board members need to be aware these contacts open the door to a staff member making an "end run" around management when the individual is dissatisfied with a management decision. As a contingency, boards should have a policy in place for addressing such issues.

Takeaway

Nonprofit boards need periodically to review and determine if the board is in compliance regarding a) duties specified by their bylaws and b) duties required of them under current law. Gaps can arise if such duties are delegated or ignored. In addition, nonprofit boards need to be alert to their often hidden responsibilities. These can range from fundraising to generating appropriate staff relationships.

CHAPTER 5

WHAT THE BOARD SHOULD EXPECT FROM MANAGEMENT

I *am indebted to Dr. Richard Leblanc of York University for the headings in this chapter and the one that fol-lows on management expectations. The headings were developed by Dr. Leblanc for his blog: "What a Board Expects from Management, and What Management Expects from a Board," January 27, 2013, York University Governance Gateway Blog. (rleblanc.apps01.yorku.ca) Dr. Leblanc's specific quotes, which can apply to either for-profit or nonprofit boards, appear in italics.*

There are five expectations the board should have of management:

No Surprises or Spin
If the CEO manages the board, or holds cards too close to the vest, this is a problem for the board.

<u>Author Comment:</u> The biggest surprise I ever received as a nonprofit board director occurred when a board's executive committee acquired, at management's suggestion and without an open discussion by the full board, a profit-making business. The agreement package presented to the board placed it in an untenable position. I resigned soon after but the remainder of the board, largely composed of senior business executives, stayed on. Why? It's a mystery to me!

Directors need to be especially alert whenever a potential change is discussed and to make certain it is fully appraised. Discussion by the full board should take place before any tentative agreement is reached.

Bad News Must Rise

Management needs to have systems, process and incentives that have full transparency and reporting...without any spin.

<u>Author Comment:</u> In a world of instant communication and ever evolving social media platforms, operational transparency for every nonprofit, regardless of size or mission, is critical. A nonprofit director should assume any significant misstep by the nonprofit will be reported in the digital world and may even spread virally across the world before a board has a chance to meet. Communication about important negative information can't wait for board meetings. Of

course, management can easily communicate by phone and email with board members, send out press releases, or hold a press conference to get its message out to the public. Yet increasingly nonprofits are also weighing when to use social media to get quickly in front of key stakeholders. Recognize that use of social media platforms is still a "Wild West" and that both large and small nonprofits are struggling with how to "tame" it. Meeting that challenge requires having both human and financial resources.

With today's ever tightening budgets many nonprofits simply don't have the resources to conduct the necessary experimentation required. When weighing communication options utilizing social media, consider fiscal resources first.

Deep (Fiscal) Expertise

The board needs to overview the abilities of financial personnel with significant care. While the board must delegate the selection of the management team to the chief executive, it must be comfortable that the CFO is appropriate to the needs of the organization. For example, in some nonprofit organizations, the CFO only needs to be able to generate accurate financial statements on time. In others, he/she needs to be able to do creative financial planning. CEOs have to be competent enough to be able to certify that the finances are in order.

Author Comment: I am very familiar with a story involving a nonprofit CFO who kept post-poning monthly reports on accounts receivable from clients. Neither the CEO nor board members demanded the report since they wanted to be "good about it" and not pressure the CFO. When the report finally was submitted, board members realized the CFO had been listing uncollectable accounts as assets. This error required a restatement of the financials for several years and the engagement of costly outside forensic accountants to review all financial transactions. As a result both the CEO and the CFO lost their jobs.

Having the right skills on staff is essential. Nonprofit boards must be certain that the organization's management group has the proper array of strengths, especially in the finance and accounting areas. Recognize that many chief executives have risen through a career path, which took them through service operations but often without exposure to financial and accounting experiences or possibly even prior for-profit or nonprofit board experience.

Visibility of Management Thinking

Management's thinking and assumption(s) need to be fully transparent to the board and open to critique...the board should (also) see what was rejected and why.

Author Comment #1: An example of where nonprofit board members are often "kept in the dark" is compensation of staff. Salary schedules are often reported via a CEO-provided document with the CEO simply commenting "our salaries are competitive."

Author Comment #2: An entirely different approach is where a nonprofit board has its CEO present alternatives on an issue (e.g., new program, extended service hours), without the CEO explaining assumptions or reasoning, for board decision. A weak CEO can even prefer this process because it allows delegation of responsibility upward to the board. If the outcome is not successful, the CEO's excuse can then be, "The board told me to do it." Although countless nonprofits still perpetuate this approach, it is an absolute throwback to the days when an organization was young and board members literally ran everything.

Author Note: "Visibility of thinking" is actually a concept that should also extend to board executive committees (or other committees) that make recommendations to the full board. For example, an executive committee or small compensation committee might recommend X% raise for the CEO, without giving the full board details on total compensation or the rationale for it. Transparent thinking behind the recommendation is essential! Unfortunately, even though

CEO compensation is public information that must be reported on the IRS 990 Form, some directors are too embarrassed to ask for specifics and others avoid critical questions because they don't want to appear unsupportive of the CEO or of committee members' work.

Full Information
There should be no information funneling or blockage of any sort

Author Comment: For many years as a director on nonprofit and for-profit boards, I have used and promoted the following three-step process to allow board members to have occasional contact with staff below the management level.

1) The board should have access to any piece of information or to any personnel to do its job. Sarbanes-Oxley, a federal law enacted in 2002 that requires corporate transparency for business corporations, has had an impact on nonprofits that want to adhere to its philosophy. A commonly accepted wisdom is that directors have an obligation or a right to openly communicate with individuals at all levels who may have pertinent information.
2) Complete the communication above with the full knowledge of the CEO.

3) Share the information developed with senior management without divulging the identities of specific individuals.

Takeaway

To be effective, nonprofit boards need to insist (enforce, if needed) their top five from management – no surprises or spin; bad news must rise; fiscal expertise; management thinking made visible; access to full information!

CHAPTER 6

WHAT MANAGEMENT SHOULD
EXPECT FROM THE BOARD

*A*gain, *I am indebted to Dr. Richard Leblanc of York University for the headings and italicized quotes in this chapter, which apply to both for-profit and nonprofit boards. For more information about Dr. Leblanc, see the previous chapter, What the Board Should Expect from Management.*

Management should have eight expectations of board directors.

Candor

Directors need to be candid and speak their mind in board meetings, not have hidden agendas, nor speak inconsistently offline. If directors are inconsistent, it can cause a schism in board-management relations and trust. The board should speak with one voice and not send mixed messages to management.

Author Comment: From my field experience I know of a nonprofit board that was split over how to deal with a newly hired CEO who had encountered problems managing staff. One board faction wanted to give him more time to heal the situation and the other argued for dismissal. The ultimate outcome was dismissal, but a schism between the board and staff had already developed and remained for decades.

A nonprofit board not only needs to send consistent messages to management, but also to staff. In addition, director candor encompasses the following:

- When you make statements outside the boardroom they need to mirror those made inside the boardroom.
- When you consider proposals before the board it's wrong to "rubber stamp" one just because it's put forth by a "strong" individual (e.g., CEO, board chair, major donor on board, influential director).

Integrity and Independence

Directors cannot be self-interested, nor use their position to self-deal. If a director promotes management capture to occur by currying favor with management, this will undermine management-board relations. Management is entitled to directors preserving their independence and not placing management in compromising positions.

Author Comment: It is important to note another potential side to self-dealing if directors don't maintain integrity and independence. For example, one CEO was able to exert powerful influence over her board by playing to board members' egos and providing special social occasions. Although the CEO apparently had a highly authoritative management style, directors ignored staff complaints. In addition, directors approved a salary for the CEO that was far above market rate. When confronted with the facts after investigation by the state attorney general, the board refused to do anything about the issues, and was subsequently removed by legal means.

On almost all nonprofit boards, members are independent. But it is critical to remember that each nonprofit board as a unit is the group responsible for overviewing the organization for community or industry stakeholders. Director self-interest (or allowing CEO self-interest to flourish) has no role to play in this process.

Trust and Confidence

Management gets demoralized when they feel the board lacks trust or confidence in them.

Author Comment: Because many nonprofit directors have professional experience with large business concerns, members of most boards aren't familiar with the kinds of constraints nonprofits encounter. As a result, I've often found, there are directors who tend to view nonprofit managers as less competent than their counterparts in the private sector. In reality, nonprofit managers may have more management field experience than many of the board's own directors, especially if their careers have been as sole contributors (e.g., attorneys, professors, medical specialists).

If there is no trust by the full board in the CEO, then the board simply has the wrong one, and the CEO must go. But otherwise, board directors, management and staff all need to respect the work that the other groups accomplish. If there is a lack of respect for any of the three, the value of the nonprofit's work will be diminished.

Knowledge

Management expects directors to invest the time to understand the (nonprofit's) business fully, especially if they are not (familiar with the nonprofit's work). Otherwise, these directors will be of limited use to management strategically and their opinions will not be taken seriously nor be credible. Management (also) gets frustrated by dated, legacy directors who have outlived their usefulness.

Author Comment: All voting nonprofit directors need to "drill down" in the organization, within an established board contacting process, to become acquainted with the contributions of key staff. Unfortunately not everyone understands this message! It's especially important for directors to understand the mission and how to overview the quality of its execution. This often requires contact with key staff below the management level. In addition, directors must be able to understand the principles of fund accounting — a responsibility that's often difficult for business executives because it isn't part of the business world. Finally directors must develop a robust understanding of their governance responsibilities.

Most directors know when they are just taking up a seat on a nonprofit board, shouldn't run for a new term and instead make room for "new blood" on the board, or should accept an invitation to join the honorary board, if it exists. But when a director isn't aware it's time to move off the board, it's almost always the case that the board chair and CEO do know. The chair should initiate a private conversation with the reluctant-to-leave director, usually around the time potential board candidates are being vetted.

Direction

A good — and smart — CEO wants a strong board. A board of directors should direct management as and when necessary to prevent the CEO from making that one big mistake.

Author Comment: If there is to be a basis for CEO entrepreneurship, which is ideal on virtually all nonprofit boards, three "principles of understanding" need to exist between board and CEO.

1. No one does his or her job perfectly, and the CEO needs the latitude to take prudent risks, some of which will be mistakes.
2. The board should formally counter decisions management makes only when necessary to prevent the CEO from making that one big mistake.
3. The board represents a larger group of stakeholders that is looking to the board for reasonable and prudent results.

React in a Measured Way

If there are leaks, or the board is constantly critical, the CEO will not bring ideas or concepts, or his or her real thinking to the board, but only a polished crystal ball for board approval.

Author's Comment: There is an acceptable way to express criticism and an unacceptable way. Stating your criticism clearly and succinctly is recommended. If appropriate, displaying a sense of humor can be helpful. But what matters more than anything is tone!

Most directors walk out of board meetings without thinking about how a CEO will convey information about the board discussion to his or her senior staff. Inevitably the tone the board used with the CEO will be conveyed (or at least clearly indicated) in the remarks the CEO subsequently makes to staff. Tone has a way of showing (or not showing) respect, and a negative tone will have a negative impact on the organization.

Meeting Preparation

Management expects each director to arrive fully briefed and ready to discuss (issues) and should be able to rely on (directors for making this effort). Otherwise, the engagement level degrades and gets sidetracked.

<u>Author Comment:</u> Although being prepared sounds like a "no brainer" it is actually a continuing problem for both for-profit and nonprofit boards. Most board meetings typically last for 90 to 120 minutes before individuals on the board start excusing themselves to get back to their offices. Any meeting time taken up extensively reviewing what is in board members' briefing packets is precious time that is lost to discussion and decision-making.

But if the board isn't getting briefing material (or the right kind of information) from management far enough in advance, it must let the CEO know what's needed and when.

Asking Good Questions

Lastly, management knows that the best directors ask the best questions that cause them to really think.

<u>Author Comment:</u> While every board member has an obligation to ask the best questions possible, each also must be ready to ask "what if" questions. Nonprofit directors have a more difficult time than their for-profit counterparts in asking "what if" questions since most aren't intimately involved in the nonprofit's field. The CEO does need to outline for directors current and future challenges for both existing and future opportunities.

Takeaway

Management's eight expectations aren't something that can be mandated. But the quality of the board-management relationship, board decision-making, and organizational governance is absolutely linked to them. Pay attention to your board, and you will know if they do, in fact, define how your board operates.

BEWARE POTENTIAL PITFALLS

CHAPTER 7

NONPROFIT CULTURE PRESENTS CHALLENGES

T he median tenure of a nonprofit board member can be estimated, based on current data, to be between four and six years,[5] which means "director turnover" is quite common. Many new volunteers don't have an understanding of nonprofit culture, but they can acclimate faster to board practices and priorities — saving themselves valuable "onboarding" time and frustration — if they know these key cultural lessons.

- *Mission Is Impact*
    The central mission of every corporate board is to make money for shareholders, but nonprofit organizations have diverse missions commonly framed in terms of "impact." While corporations can report financials on a regular basis and show bottom line results, nonprofits traditionally

struggle to measure mission impact tied to terminology such as "enhancing quality of life, providing opportunities, or advocating successfully."

Meeting that elusive nonprofit challenge — actually measuring impact in order to assess mission fulfillment — is becoming even more challenging today. Nonprofit CEOs and boards are being pushed by foundations and government agencies to move from only providing "outcomes" data (e.g., clients served, services provided) to providing impact data (e.g., what serving clients achieved, which services made what differences for which populations). That's because outcomes and impacts are not necessarily related. A program with seemingly great outcomes might, for example, have little to no impact. Conversely, a nonprofit working with a hard-to-serve population might have seemingly poor outcomes, but make substantial impact.

- *Measuring Impact*

    In order to close the gap between a nonprofit's ability to deliver impact data and what recipients of the data actually seek, rigorous evaluations could be very helpful. Such evaluations, however, can be difficult and time-intensive to complete, and usually are financially out of reach for small- and medium-sized nonprofits. For nonprofits without the resources for such evaluations, the author suggests the following experimental approach. It uses imperfect metrics (i.e., anecdotal, subjective, interpretative), and requires agreement and trust between nonprofits and the recipients of their data.

How to Get to Impact Assessment

Agree on relevant impacts — Use metrics that reflect organization-related impacts. These should focus on a desired change in the nonprofit's universe, rather than process activities or efforts.

Agree on measurement approaches — These can range from personal interviews to comparisons of local results with national data.

Agree on specific indicators — Outside of available data (e.g., financial results, membership numbers), nonprofits should designate behavioral impacts clients should achieve. Avoid adding other indicators simply because they are "easily developed" or "would be interesting to examine." Keep the focus on the targeted behavioral outcomes.

Agree on judgment rules — Board and management need to agree, at the outset, upon metric numbers for each specific indicator contributing to the desired strategic objective. If appropriate, board and management can also agree on specific values that are "too high" or "too low."

<u>Assess organizational impact</u> —
Determine how many specific program
objectives have reached impact levels.

The steps above closely follow the philosophy of
lean experimentation that is being suggested for
profit-making and nonprofit organizations[6] as
a way of using imperfect metrics to obtain impact data from clients or stakeholders over time.
Under a lean approach, as long as the organization garners some positive insights after each
iteration (even if starting with a small sample),
the approach leads to improved measurement
and increased comfort with the advantages and
limitations of using these metrics.

- *A Slower Pace*
  Compared with corporate boards, the pace of
  the decision process on nonprofit boards is de-
  cidedly slower, and there are numerous reasons
  why. Some common examples:
  - The nonprofit's charter may have established
    requirements that preclude hasty and poten-
    tially unwise decisions — by mandating a
    period of deliberation before an action is for-
    mally voted upon.
  - The board may recognize the organization
    doesn't have the staff needed to implement a
    proposed change quickly.

○ The nonprofit may have had to defer action due to lack of quorums at successive board meetings.

- *Get or Give Obligations*

  Many nonprofits ask board members to help generate and/or make annual donations within the parameters of their personal resources. Often directors are urged to make a "stretch" gift, make their largest donation to the organization, or seek contributions from others. Some directors resist this type of pressure, but even if a nonprofit has a development staff, board members are still responsible for pursuing funds by every appropriate means.

  Being responsible includes being prepared or helping others prepare prior to making a solicitation. In particular, don't overlook the responsibility to make certain that the CEO and development director (and any others involved) are well prepared when approaching a potential business donor. The author's recommended approach follows.

How to Engage Business Donors

Do Your Homework — The individual(s) meeting a potential business donor must know a great deal about the business. The worst possible opening is, "Tell me about what 'X' produces." That statement alone shows the solicitor(s) have no interest in the business environment in which the firm operates. In the Internet age there is no excuse for such a lapse. When homework has been done, the conversation opener might be, "How's business been recently?" The discussion that follows then can be about the donor's industry trends and challenges, establishing a level of comfort for the potential donor.

Tell What the Nonprofit Can Do for the Donor — Sophisticated development officers have ways of asking this important question in honest, forthright ways.

> *Example:* University Soliciting a Business — "We can suggest capable entry-level employees for the firm."

Show the Nonprofit Has a Business Posture — Business people want to know a nonprofit is both well managed and fulfills a human service, professional or social need. That can mean working into the discussion some key, but seemingly basic information. For example, if your top paid leader carries the title executive director (ED), understand this title puzzles many in the business world. The goal is to show, directly or indirectly, the scope of the ED's responsibilities. Other tips:

○ Show the nonprofit's mission is viable, is being carefully shepherded, and the organization doesn't engage in mission creep, but stays abreast of potential opportunities.

○ Clarify that an achievable business plan is available to the donor.

○ Demonstrate that you have a well-managed internal structure that can achieve impacts for clients. Business leaders are very aware that process goals can be met without achieving desired impacts.

○ Share specific mission developments and successes. Remember, this is not one-size-fits-all. Tailor the type of information delivered to your target audience, since different developments and achievements resonate with different audiences.

▪ *Board Chair, CEO and Staff Relationships*

In every nonprofit, this trio is at the heart of the organization. There are, however, some cultural breakdowns in internal relationships that can be disruptive to the organization.

The nonprofit's <u>board chair</u> is generally more important than his or her counterpart in the private sector. That can make others in the boardroom hesitant to challenge the chair's leadership. However, when there is reason for a director to take issue, the director should do so. Otherwise progress for the organization can be impeded and the director may be helping the board earn the moniker "rubber stamp board."

The <u>CEO</u> is the key person responsible for implementing a nonprofit's high-performance culture. If the CEO is doing a C or B grade job a board will frequently resist making a change. After all, "If it's not broken, why fix it?" On boards where the cast of members shifts frequently, typically there is a pull toward maintaining the status quo simply because it's less disruptive. Yet having a CEO who's doing just a "good enough" job is not always in the best interest of the organization. A new CEO may be who's needed to stimulate positive change.

<u>Staff</u> members in nonprofits are well attuned to the frequent rotations of board personnel. If a continually shifting board means constantly shifting priorities, staff members' work and morale will suffer.

Takeaway

When a new director is acclimated to the unique challenges of nonprofit culture, serving on the board can provide

an exceptionally rewarding experience — whether helping to serve people with significant needs, enhancing the
impact of professional and trade associations, or adding
community value.

CHAPTER 8

AVOID THESE POOR — YET ALL
TOO COMMON — PRACTICES

*T*he author is indebted to Peter Rinn, nonprofit
consultant with the Breakthrough Solutions
Group of Albuquerque, New Mexico, for publishing his list of weak nonprofit board practices.

Based on extensive experience as a nonprofit board
director, board chair and consultant, the author discusses
the practices on Rinn's list that the author has found can
present the biggest obstacles to board progress.

Dumbing down board recruitment

Far too often, nominating committees extend invitations to potential board candidates
while trumpeting the benefits and not stress-
ing the responsibilities of serving on nonprofit
boards. Likewise, candidates often accept board
positions before they have done sufficient due

diligence. At a minimum, the candidate should meet with the CEO and board chair. Issues to be clarified include meeting schedules, "give/get" policies and time expectations. In addition, if the candidate is seriously interested, he or she should ask for copies of the board meeting minutes for one year, the latest financials, and the latest IRS Form 990.

Overlooking the continued absence of board members at board, strategic and planning meetings

The bylaws of many nonprofits include provisions for dropping board members who don't meet attendance criteria. Taking such action, however, is difficult to execute because of interpersonal conflicts that can potentially arise.

> *Example:* A nonprofit had a director who contributed financially but didn't attend any meetings. When the board requested his resignation a year before his term expired, the director refused. Not wanting to create conflict, the board kept him on its roster, and a year later sent him a note acknowledging the end of his term.

Taking the "nice guy" approach is not the professional action required by the bylaws. The appropriate solution is for the board chair (not the

CEO) to have a private conversation with such a director. The chair needs to deliver a "tough love" message on behalf of the board.

Taking a board action without conducting enough due diligence to determine whether the transaction is in the nonprofit's best interest
Consider the following scenarios:

Scenario 1: A contractor didn't perform as agreed. After an influential director raises the issue of whether it's "appropriate" to legally challenge a local business person, the board decides it won't do so. No one, however, raises the issue that in being "nice" the directors may become legally liable if someone is subsequently injured as a result of their inaction.

Scenario 2: A nonprofit has property that's no longer needed. Board members agree to sell the property to the spouse of a board member for less than the market rate. This is an example of being involved in providing an "excess benefit," which violates the federal Intermediate Sanctions Act (IRS Section 4958). A board member might have his or her personal taxes increased if found in violation of the Act.

Some boards and their members need to be reminded regularly about their "due-care" responsibilities, and a good time to do so is when board members are asked to sign conflict of interest statements. Signing the statements annually should be standard practice on nonprofit boards. Unfortunately, all too often, that's not the case.

Overselling the protection of D&O insurance and laws limiting the liability of directors

Directors and officers (D&O) liability insurance, in general terms, covers for-profit or nonprofit directors and officers for claims made against them while they are serving on a board or as an officer of an organization. The importance of a nonprofit having a D&O policy, even a small one, can't be overstated. While working as a consultant the author encountered a nonprofit that had operated for 17 years without a D&O policy, even though it had an annual budget of $500,000 and oversaw real estate valued at $24 million! Every director should be knowledgeable about the potential personal liabilities involved with his or her board position. Too often, directors just assume their nonprofit's D&O insurance policy covers a full range of situations.

Allowing board members to ignore their financial obligations to the nonprofit

To assess board interest in a nonprofit, foundations and other funders like to know that every board member makes a financial contribution within his or her means or participates in the organization's "give/get" program. Expectations of the director should be addressed when each board member is initially recruited so that the person fully understands his or her financial obligation.

Allowing board members to be re-elected to the board, despite bylaw term limitations

Succession planning needs to be a yearly process not just for a CEO but also for the board itself. When very little thought has been given to a board succession plan, sometimes boards think the only individual who can replace a termed-out director is that very same director. Succession planning can also get pushed to the side when boards are facing a lot of problems, but such planning really can't wait until there is a crisis. It has to be ongoing, every year. The one exception to allowing board members to be re-elected despite term limitations should occur if the bylaws allow a board chair, if scheduled for rotation, an extra year or two to serve as chairperson.

Allowing ignorance and poor practices to exist keeps leadership in control

Changing leadership and practice is difficult enough in the for-profit environment, but even more so for nonprofit organizations. As long as current revenues cover expenditures, poor leadership and practices can continue in a non-profit for a long period of time. They can even become part of the organization's culture, occasionally even due to low expectations of management and staff by board members. It's critical that nonprofit leadership be thoroughly examined every year.

NOTE: Based on the author's experience, here are a few more practices to avoid.

Failing to delegate sufficient managerial responsibility to the CEO

Many nonprofit boards micromanage operational activities for years or even decades — long after a nonprofit has passed the embryo stage when volunteer directors must actually run the organization. Instead of policy discussions on mature nonprofits' boards, for example, there may be tedious debates about operational issues (e.g., minor adjustment of fees, internal process changes, supplies vendor selection) The author even knows one board that refused to share its latest strategic plan with its newly hired executive director!

Engaging a weak local CEO because the board wants to avoid moving expenses

Be certain local applicants are vetted as carefully as others and that the cost of relocation isn't the prime driver for selecting a local candidate.

Selecting a board chair on the basis of his or her personality and appearance

What's really important is that the board chair has managerial and organizational competence. Because nonprofit boards must draw director candidates from a broad base of backgrounds, the author has found boards typically have no more than one or two members who are able *and willing* to be the kind of leaders best suited to fill the board chair position.

Takeaway

Directors need to have a passion for the nonprofit's mission. Just as important is having the wisdom to help the board perform with professionalism.

CHAPTER 9

The boundary line that exists between board and management needs serious respect. To avoid crossing the line, board chairs and CEOs must have trust in one another and be certain that both sides understand the boundary. If the board is spending more time weighing details of operations than it is on planning, strategy and assessment it's a sure sign the board is "micromanaging" and has crossed the boundary line.

- *What is the board's boundary?*

    "Nose in, fingers out" is the commonly used refrain to guide board members' involvement with nonprofit operations. What that means is the board has an obligation to overview management outcomes and their impacts, but must avoid micromanaging the operations that achieve them.

Because micromanagement seems to be in the DNA of so many nonprofit boards – and is more immediately gratifying than policy or strategy — crossing the boundary line poses particular danger.

> Example: A nonprofit board designated the CEO as the person responsible for press relations. A well-meaning board member contacts a print media outlet and tells a story about the organization that's not accurate. The organization publicly retracts the story. Board chair and CEO emphasize to directors that all press contacts must be channeled to the CEO.

- *What is the CEO's boundary?*
On the operations side, strong and experienced CEOs can tend to be overly impatient and can easily make strategic or policy decisions that are the responsibility of the board.

> Example: A nonprofit's CEO signs a five-year lease for office space without obtaining formal board approval. Although the board agrees with the CEO that the space is needed, the total obligation is $3,000 a year. The board chair tells the CEO the lease is a long-term obligation and should

have been approved by the board before he signed it. The CEO argues he signs larger contracts in the normal course of the nonprofit's business. Ultimately they agree the CEO crossed the boundary and the board now has to approve the contract retroactively.

Frequently Asked Questions

Q. *Is there ever an exception that allows the board to cross the line?*

A. There's a need for a micromanaging board only when a nonprofit (or for-profit) is in the start-up phase. Since financial and human resources are typically modest, at best, directors often need to assume some responsibilities usually executed by paid staff. The CEO's managerial responsibilities may also include low-level operational duties (e.g., installing furniture, calling suppliers) at start-up.

Q. *What are the long-term implications of having a micromanaging board after the start-up phase?*

A. Micromanagement can become imbedded in the DNA of the organization's decision-making, and behavioral patterns emerge that, over time, negatively impact the health of the organization. Some of the potential dangers:

- If the board's mandates fail, directors can quietly blame management for poor implementation. Eventually such failures stunt the organization's development or cause it to fail.
- Less competent managers are attracted to executive positions when there's a micromanaging board.
- Decisions get delegated upward, since even small decisions need board review, if not approval. That restricts managerial initiative, creativity, critical thinking and strategic planning.
- Impacts and outcomes may be minimal, but this isn't readily recognized by the community or sponsoring organization. As long as income meets expenses each year, the board doesn't note any long-term red flags.

Q. *How is the boundary line developed appropriately?*

A. Delineating the line can occur in two different ways. The first is to detail the obligations in the bylaws and/or job descriptions. This approach, however, can lead to confusion in some situations or to overregulation. The second option, and the method recommended by the author, is to list the functions of the board and then allow the CEO and board chair to clarify the boundary as situations arise. If boundary crossing becomes too frequent (and, of course, no one can do a job perfectly 100% of the time), then the overall role of governance needs to be reassessed.

Q. *Is there a sample statement of board responsibilities that can be used as a guide?*

A. The board:

Directs management

    a) Establishes, with management, long-term organizational objectives and impacts

    b) Sets overall policies affecting strategies designed to achieve objectives and impacts

    c) Hires the CEO

Judges management outcomes and impacts

    a) Evaluates short- and long-term management performance

    b) Determines whether policies are being carried out and goals and impacts achieved

Approves management actions

    a) Critically reviews and approves/disapproves proposals in policy areas

        Examples: major capital expenditures, pension plan modifications

    b) Provides formal recognition and acceptance of executive decisions if related to operations within specified budget guidelines

Advises management

    a) Acts in an advisory or consultative capacity on operations at the request of management

Receives information from management

    a) Regularly review reports on the organization
        Examples: performance, program development, external pressures, concerns

Acts as a resource to management

    a) Helps keep the organization attuned to the environment in which it operates (e.g., public, community and industrial relations)

Partners with management to develop funding

    a) Several board members, the CEO and the development director, if available, need to serve as a well-coordinated team

Q. *When is using the author's recommended approach to delineate the boundary especially effective?*

A. If both board members and the CEO are "mature" — governmentally and managerially speaking — this approach is particularly effective. Maturity, in this sense, means there is a high degree of respect for the expertise of the CEO, directors see their role as overview of management and, working with management, making policy and strategic decisions.

Q. *What are the major benefits of this approach?*
A. There are three.

1. The board chair can eliminate agenda items that are operational details and avoid discussions at board meetings that drift into operational minutiae.
2. Using this model attracts individuals who view the role of board director broadly and want to contribute their talents effectively and efficiently.
3. Management has significant accountability, and therefore the board must provide robust assessment of outcomes and impacts (not processes).

Q. *Board members need to be informed about operations in order to overview them, but how?*
A. Various methods can be used but keeping important information flowing to the board is critical to having a high-performing nonprofit, and it is a significant responsibility of the CEO. Here are some practical suggestions that can be used or adapted.

- Weekly board chair/CEO conference calls — Directors who have time can join the call, and the CEO overviews what's happening in operations. A few days later the CEO sends a brief email to all board members highlighting important events that took place during the week.

- <u>Staff deliver frequent, short presentations to the board</u> — This is a more traditional approach but in practice can be an ineffective one. The problem can be that the staff member is so enthusiastic that he or she presents for far too long, or that board members raise "micromanagement" type questions that extend the presentation. Two solutions exist. The CEO can meet with the staff person ahead of the meeting to ensure the presentation is succinct and within the allotted time limit. The board chair should suggest to directors that detailed questions can best be answered "offline."

- <u>"Consent Agenda" approach</u> — With a consent agenda, routine and previously agreed upon items are organized together and then, hopefully, approved as a group. If one or more directors question an item in the group, it is placed on the agenda for the next board meeting. This process eliminates time-consuming separate discussion for every item.

- <u>CEO quarterly informal meetings with directors</u> — In these one-on-one discussions the CEO can discuss the more "entrepreneurial or wild ideas" that might need testing and update directors on operational decisions in greater detail. Some of the meetings can happen quite informally, such as before or after a committee meeting or after board meetings. Others can occur at scheduled times or appropriate events. Obviously the CEO needs to meet with the board chair more often. The executive's assistant should track all meetings and have authority to make new appointments to maintain the schedule. If the board is a national one, meeting less frequently or having scheduled phone calls can work well. One veteran CEO the author knows often meets with two board members at a time, pairing a long-serving member with a recently appointed director.

Takeaway

Nonprofit boards must hire a top paid executive (regardless of title used) in whom the board can place a high degree of trust. But that does not negate the board's responsibility to annually and robustly evaluate the top leader and the organization's performance!

CHAPTER 10

BEING AN ATTENTIVE
BOARD MEMBER REALLY MATTERS

F iduciary responsibility refers to the relationship between a board director and the body for whom the
director acts. Not being vigilant about that responsibility could potentially be very expensive for a director.

The personal cost of director inattentiveness was
made clear in 2015 as part of a federal appeals court case
known as the Lemington Home decision, which resulted
in board liability costs of $2.25 million and additional
punitive damages for some defendants. The decision
was the last stage in a nearly decade-long court battle
tied to the bankruptcy of a small, historically significant
nonprofit nursing home that had served a predominantly
minority community in Pittsburgh.

The Lemington Home decision is viewed as having important implications for nonprofits, regardless of the size

or type of organization. Why? Because prior to Lemington Home there was a dearth of reported legal decisions specifically identifying board actions or inactions that establish a breach of fiduciary duty. The jury in Lemington Home found board members failed to respond to clear indications of executive incompetence or mismanagement, and didn't maintain basic elements of corporate governance (e.g., improper minute taking, poor attendance at board meetings, officer position [e.g., treasurer] left vacant.[7]

Are there other examples of board inattentiveness? Here are some the author has encountered that were not subject to personal liabilities.

Failure to Assess Staff Realities

Concerned with the authoritarian style of a newly appointed executive director, an agency's social work staff complained directly to board members. Wanting to avoid negative publicity for the organization, the board decided to give the new executive a second chance to improve relations. However, a local electrical workers' union learned of the discord, and without the board being aware, took steps to unionize the agency's social work staff. After six difficult months of internal turmoil, staff voted to unionize. The new leader was fired by the board for failing to develop positive relationships, the organization's United Way funding was temporarily jeopardized, and directors suffered reputational loss.

Failure to Have an Audit Committee

Many nonprofit boards don't have an audit committee, including many who are required to have one under the laws of their own state. This failure is especially prevalent when nonprofit board members believe that too rigorous an examination indicates the board doesn't trust management and staff. The other extreme reported in the media is where a CEO is clearly guilty of an offense, but the board refuses to take proper action and state authorities act to replace the board members.

Failure to Meet the Basics of Compliance

For a nonprofit board, these are the basics of compliance.

a) All directors must be thoroughly familiar with duties of due care (e.g., conflict of interest, need for D&O insurance) their responsibilities related to IRS Form 990 and the Intermediate Sanctions Act, and the fundamentals of fund accounting for financial reports.

b) All nonprofit personnel involved with finances must take, at a minimum, two weeks of vacation annually.

c) The board and top management must be serious about punishing individuals who use organizational resources for personal use.

d) Board members must sign a conflict of interest statement annually.

e) All non-routine expenditures over XX must be signed by two board members.

f) All individuals with access to the organization's cash are to be covered by a surety bond policy.

g) The board needs to change auditing firms or the partner in charge of the account every three to five years.

Failure to Protect Board Colleagues

Some boards refuse to purchase directors and officers (D&O) liability insurance. The faulty rationale behind such refusals is often, "we're very close to the finances, and fraud can't happen here." In one scenario the board was responsible for more than $20 million in assets and a $700,000 reserve fund, and had an annual operating budget exceeding $350,000.

It's certainly worthwhile noting that if a $1 million D&O policy was applied toward a $2.25 million fine (the amount specified in the Lemington Homes decision) the 15 directors on this board would personally be responsible for the balance – or about $83,000 per director.

Failure to Approve a Whistle-Blowing Process

Whistle-blowing hotlines are very common today, but some boards shy from establishing them for fear they will be interpreted as the board being distrustful of staff. This can be a short-sighted view, although a very human one. In the long run, experience shows some trusted individuals can be identified as criminals (e.g., Madoff). From a cost-benefit perspective, it's wise board policy to have an established whistle-blowing process. Not having one is negligence that, in the long run, can lead to board conflict, require additional board meetings and cause personal rifts with colleagues or friends.

Takeaway

As volunteers, nonprofit board members too often hesitate to be thorough when questioning or evaluating the organization and the CEO. Drop the hesitancy. Being attentive matters!

CHAPTER 11

To Avoid Fraud,
Boards Must Take Action

Scams can happen anytime there is opportunity, and nonprofits — regardless of their reputation — aren't immune. One scenario that garnered headlines recently involved a top executive of a nonprofit who worked with various vendors to inflate prices and then split the excess portion of payments with the vendors. Investigation into the practice revealed substantial billings, over a multi-year time period, were involved in the scheme.

Two Committees Are Required

There are two specific committees that the board must not only have, but also charge with specific tasks. These tasks are designed to help reduce fraud.

- *Finance Committee*
  The committee's tasks include:
  a) Reviewing the overall results of a yearly independent audit conducted by an outside auditor.
  b) Overseeing executive compensation, pension benefits and other finance activities.

- *Audit Committee*
  This is a common board standing or subcommittee for both for-profit and non-profit organizations. It's prudent to exclude from this committee any directors with strong social, family or political links to management personnel. The directors who do serve should be reasonably financially competent, with at least one member with a strong finance background being able to overview audit issues in detail. Major tasks are to:
  a) Conduct a yearly review of conflict-of-interest policies.
  b) Ensure all board members and employees sign a conflict-of-interest statement.
  c) Assure that new hires are vetted for honesty.
  d) Meet every four to six months.
  e) Make sure than a certified audit is completed at least every two years — ideally once a year, if possible.

The Full Board Must Take Three Actions

To avoid fraud the board must:

- *Engage an External Auditing Firm*

  It used to be common for managers to select the external auditing firm with "rubber stamp" approval by the board. In today's more vigilant environment, the board must be more involved. Hiring the auditing firm should be a partnership effort between management and the board. The task ranks alongside the selection of a CEO in terms of how serious it is. The board Audit Committee should review the following information when hiring the auditing firm:

  o The nonprofit audit experience of the firm that will conduct the audit

  o The auditing firm's history and client list

  o The proportion of the firm's clients that are nonprofits

  o The size of the firm and its ability to serve the organization well

  o The estimated costs of each audit

  o The auditing firm's suggestion for a financial consulting firm should the nonprofit be in need of such counsel

- *Meet with External Auditors*

  At the time the Audit Committee meets with the external auditors, the organization's

CFO and other key financial personnel will attend. However, at some point in the meeting, the full board needs to meet with the auditors without the CEO, CFO and other managers present. This is the time for board members to ask the auditors, "Do you have anything to tell the board without management present?" This gives auditors the opportunity to report any concerns that need board consideration (e.g., unusual travel, entertainment or other expenses, transactions that raise red flags). At this private session, Audit Committee members also need to take the opportunity to raise questions about the professional competence of the nonprofit's internal financial personnel.

- *Develop a Conversation with External Auditors*

  Typically a nonprofit Audit Committee will have only one or two members with the expertise to formulate detailed technical questions for external auditors. Thus, it is important that every board member be familiar with the following topics and be able to pose critical questions.

  a) Are controls adequate? The organization's control system needs to be divided into operating functions. Then, each operating function must be performed by someone different so that each person checks others' work.

b) <u>Are financial records accurate?</u> External auditors must certify that these records are in proper form: financial statements, management contracts, sales of major assets, bonus payments, and long-term leases.

c) <u>Are activities and expenditures properly authorized?</u> For example, have any extensive changes in plans been approved by the board? Have major expenses been properly budgeted? Have travel costs over a prescribed level been approved by a senior officer? Depending on the size of the nonprofit, do expenditures over a certain amount require two signatures from senior officers?

d) <u>Do all reported assets actually exist?</u> This question is especially important if the organization holds any physical assets at a distance from its main offices.

e) <u>Is the organization performing any activities that might endanger its tax-exempt status?</u> Smaller nonprofits sometimes let licenses or even tax-exempt certificates lapse. It's vital to certify that such documents are current and that taxable income and charitable donations are reported separately.

f) <u>Is the organization paying its payroll taxes, sales taxes and license fees on time?</u> Does the nonprofit file its financial reports, like the IRS 990 report, on time? Many instances of fraud involve failure to report and pay employee withholding taxes.

Takeaway

The potential for fraud needs intense board attention because fraud is a pervasive cancer in the nonprofit environment. Cases of fraud within a nonprofit undermine both the organization's good work and good name. The realization that board members give serious attention to the issue of fraud, in and of itself, may help deter someone from trying to use agency resources to their own advantage.

THE BOARD'S CRITICAL JOBS

CHAPTER 12

THE MOST IMPORTANT JOB IS
CEO SELECTION AND OVERVIEW

Finding the best possible person to act as CEO of a nonprofit is rarely easy. Yet at some point in time, the board of every nonprofit in the nation must tackle the job, one that requires the very best work a board can do. CEO selection and the board's subsequent overview of the person chosen for the position are discussed below. "Onboarding the CEO" is addressed immediately after that, both because it is integral to a smooth transition and because it is an area where far too many nonprofit boards are falling short.

CEO Selection and Overview Guidelines

- *Recruit widely*

    Develop a rigorous vetting process. Before the search begins, make certain that potential internal candidates have had an opportunity to demonstrate management acumen. There will be many questions asked of all candidates, but one needs to be "What are your career expectations and aspirations?" in order to ascertain whether the candidate's goals are compatible with the nonprofit's. In the end, if an internal candidate is less qualified than an external one, don't let the board decision be impacted by the fact that the internal candidate is "cheaper" to employ.

- *Understand and communicate what you expect from the partnership*
  The need for the board and CEO to operate within a partnership framework is well documented and widely accepted. At the same time, the CEO will be both senior staff manager and de facto representative of the board/staff relationship. Normal communications to the staff must be through the CEO, and the CEO can't be an insecure manager who will withhold negative information from the board.

- *After selecting the CEO, step back – but overview*
  Once the CEO is selected, the author and other leading experts argue the board's role is to stand back and let the

CEO manage, while directors overview the CEO's work. It is the board's responsibility to not let this obligation devolve into "supervising" management. In other words, the CEO should have full operational authority, and the staff shouldn't function under any hint of board micromanagement.

- *Seek appropriate organizational performance and CEO measurement*
  As explained earlier, the board must seek data and information on outcomes and impacts, not details on processes.

- *Accept that the CEO won't do his or her job perfectly*
  The board needs to be highly tolerant of inconsequential CEO mistakes. If these mistakes persist over time, the board needs to assess reasons why they continue. Major errors, of course, need immediate investigation. The board must be honest about any due diligence failings of its own that relate to the error.

- *Evaluate the CEO fairly*
  Evaluation is done in partnership by the board and CEO, not administered by a board hierarchy. Each side of the partnership must understand the "rules of the

game," where outcomes and their impacts relate to the organization's mission.

- *Partner with the CEO on fundraising*
  The CEO is the face of the organization and consequently must accept a significant responsibility for fundraising. As noted in Chapter 7, board members also have a critical role to play in fundraising.

CEO Onboarding Guidelines

Nearly half (46%) of the 214 CEOs responding to a Bridgespan Group survey published in 2014 reported getting little or no help from their boards when first taking on the position. As one executive director told the nonprofit advisory group, "The board essentially said, 'We're glad you're here. Here are the keys. We're tired.' "[8]

In order for the new leader to develop a solid base in the organization and understand its distinct climate and culture, the board must structure an approach for orienting the CEO. The orientation could take up to a year to complete, with board commitment decreasing over time. Major responsibility for the program should rest with the board chair, but also involve one or more senior board members.

Every program is tailored to the situation, but should have the following nine steps. They can be completed in sequence or concurrently.

1) <u>Develop immediate and long-term goals:</u> This process is well understood and usually is quickly accomplished.

2) <u>Review fiscal and personnel resources:</u> This step is also easy to accomplish.

3) <u>Examine current policies and procedures:</u> Although routine, this is a necessary task. Certainly the top administrative staff should be responsible for the new CEO's orientation on operating policies and procedures, and the CEO's own knowledge will deepen in the course of making operating decisions. When it comes to understanding how the board goes about setting policies, the CEO does need a formal orientation from the board chair. Together they should then establish a work plan to determine if all board policies are concise, understandable and operationally complete. Depending upon the current state, this task can be simple or require extensive revisions and additions.

4) <u>Nurture CEO/staff relationships:</u> In every organization, changes at the top spark staff insecurity and unrest. Comfortable patterns are broken and often there's resistance to change. Board members must provide strong support for needed changes. The board should also be represented at all business meetings and functions where the board traditionally participates.

5) <u>Foster board relationships:</u> An astute CEO will want to get to know the board well, and directors should expect a strong leader to assertively develop these interpersonal relationships. The CEO should meet individually with board members at their place of employment or other convenient location.

6) <u>Cultivate community or industry associations:</u> Together the board chair and CEO create a game plan designed to help the CEO develop contacts and relationships with community and industry leaders and/or other stakeholders, such as key vendors.

7) <u>Understand customers, clientele, membership and stakeholders:</u> Through informal meetings, presentations or reviews of pertinent issues, the board should strive to give the new CEO an understanding of how the products or services offered are perceived by various stakeholder groups. The CEO should then try to verify the information in visits with stakeholders. If one or more significant gaps are noted, the CEO has an obligation to review the gap(s) with the board to determine whether the current strategic plan should be modified.

8) <u>Discuss the CEO's career growth plan:</u> The board and CEO must agree on a plan

for the CEO's career development and growth, and the board should specify what it is willing to do to help the CEO with that plan.

9) <u>Develop two succession plans:</u> The first plan will cover any situation where the CEO is temporarily incapacitated, and should be developed quickly. The second covers long-term succession planning, and is revised periodically following discussions that take place every few years with the CEO and his or her direct reports.

Takeaway

Selecting and overviewing the CEO is the board's most important job. Numerous benefits accrue for boards that take the time to orient their CEO. The most significant benefit is the smooth transition that a structured orientation program promotes. As a result, power, authority, leadership and accountability are clearly understood and accepted by both the board and the new CEO. Misunderstandings and conflicts can be avoided.

CHAPTER 13

RECOGNIZE WHEN DIRECTORS
SHOULD QUESTION THE "NORM"

Every nonprofit has standard patterns of behavior that are considered normal for the organization. Given the speed with which a director moves from novice to board retiree (typically a median four to six years), and board chairs complete their service (typically one to two years) it can be a challenge to advocate for successful change that differs from long accepted norms.

Here are three nonprofit areas that call for strategic scrutiny and, if recognized by several other current board members as constraints on the future of the nonprofit, presented as opportunities to weigh options for positive change.

Time for Mission Creep?
Dedication to the organization's mission should be the board and staff's primary focus — but hard and fast

adherence to mission parameters can sometimes be an avoidance mechanism to maintain the status quo.

Field Story: For decades a human services agency offers counseling services weekdays from 9 to 5, with extended hours on Thursdays until 8 p.m. There are no emergency services. Board members have grown accustomed to the rigid service schedule and resist any change, despite the urgency of client needs. It takes a new group of board members, with the support of a new CEO, to develop a cost-effective way to provide 24/7 service.

Author Comment: Nonprofits have an obligation to keep current in addressing emerging needs, but a conservative board may have a tendency to veto a client venture that has reasonable potential. How do directors determine an initiative's positive or negative impact on the organization? By wrestling with tough questions and examining options.

Overhead vs. Development Maxim

A great many organizations follow the maxim that about 80% of a nonprofit's overall budget should be expended on direct client or customer services. When this philosophy becomes a rigid operating principle, it can override acceptance of carefully planned increases in overhead that might yield substantial increases in program budgets.

Field Story: A CEO adept at fundraising refused to engage a Chief Operating Officer, citing increased overhead as his reason. After four years of board prodding, he relented and made the appointment. The result was positive on two fronts — the CEO was able to expand his fundraising activities and the COO significantly improved internal operations.

Author Comment: When the need for a new type of staff arrangement arises, it is often hotly contested. But board members need to strive to get past rhetoric and move the organization forward.

A Rubber Stamp Board

Many boards have a tendency to be a rubber stamp for management. This can be a significant danger for nonprofit boards with a "go along to get along" culture.

Field Story: A university trustee, an alumnus, was concerned about plans to offer an MBA in an abbreviated time period. He had earned his degree in the program, and was convinced such a change would significantly diminish program quality. Not wanting to challenge management's strong recommendation for making the change, he said nothing at the board meeting where it was presented and voted upon. Later he felt guilty about his silence and talked about it with a former professor!

Author Comment: There is nothing sacred about monthly two-hour board meetings, but crowded agendas and limited Q&A time can inhibit any type of rigorous discussion. Board members who want to suggest new ideas or question accepted norms are often frustrated and discouraged from doing so. Although the traditional meeting format is rarely challenged, there are alternative options. Board meetings might be scheduled for longer periods bi-monthly, or other time arrangements can be explored. Instead of allowing time for just current updates, the format, if carefully re-structured, could accommodate substantive policy/strategy issues where board members' ideas can really be heard.

Takeaway

Ties to traditional modes of governance are hard to sever, but with sensitivity and persistence, a proactive director can help move the organization forward. He or she will need as colleagues at least several other directors who understand the importance of questioning board norms.

CHAPTER 14

BOARD AND STAFF SHOULD PARTNER
TO DEVELOP THE STRATEGIC PLAN

Maintaining a viable strategic plan is a board responsibility, but the nonprofit's staff must be employed in its development. Ideally the plan's development is a partnership between the two entities, with the CEO representing the staff and calling upon staff expertise as needed. Only in crisis situations should boards develop strategic plans on their own. These usually involve significant financial problems and/or situations where the CEO has been fired and there is no one else to provide planning leadership.

There is no single model to follow but there are some important common guidelines for every nonprofit embarking on strategic planning.

Having directors who are strategic thinkers

How successful the planning effort will be depends a great deal on whether or not the board has several directors who are strategic thinkers with experience working on strategy efforts at a high level in other environments. Consequently, these directors will be aware of the bumps in the road that are part of the process, and won't be content with substituting a broad brush "strengths, weaknesses, opportunities and threats (SWOT) analysis" for a strategic plan. In addition, they will find ways to incorporate imperfect qualitative measures into the plan, a necessary assessment for nonprofits with impacts that are difficult to measure.

Sometimes boards are largely composed of mid-level managers and independent professionals, and lack a single board member with any strategic background. That's one major reason nominating committees have to be so aware of the need to recruit some directors who are critical thinkers and know how to plan strategically.

Getting the planning process rolling

The board's experienced strategic thinkers and the CEO should meet for initial process planning, such as determining whether an outside consultant is needed to bring a neutral view into the effort. Often a consultant will act as professional facilitator and work with a steering committee that knows the mission and the environment in which the nonprofit operates.

Bringing staff who aren't on the steering committee into the planning process

Staff needs to be involved in the process at some point. Some nonprofits include a senior person on the steering committee. Others wait until basic challenges have been reviewed and then hold a board-staff retreat to obtain staff perspectives. The staff can have significant impact. Being close to daily activities, staff can provide unique perspectives on new ways to refine the mission.

Recognizing potential obstacles to implementing the plan

After the entire board and staff are reading from the same document, and it has the board's formal approval, there are potential obstacles that must be recognized. Where they exist, they have to be overcome if the plan's benefits are to be realized.

- Problems and crises will continue to arise for the organization, and opportunities will need to be addressed. How can the plan be kept in the forefront of board and management thinking?

- People key to the development of the strategic plan will rotate off the board within a few years, and the board chair under whose guidance the plan was developed will be termed out. What needs to be done to maintain focus?
- The existing CEO is skilled operationally but just doesn't do well when it comes to thinking strategically, or the CEO leaves the organization abruptly. Who will be the plan's advocate? There are two suggested solutions:

> Option 1) Endow ownership of the plan: Ideally one competent CEO (existing at the plan's adoption or as successor) will be in place for the plan's duration and can work with a series of board chairs to implement it.
>
> Given some nonprofits' board rotation policies (e.g., allowing the chair to hold office only for a year), institutional memory, however, may be fragile. Also having a strategically weak CEO can make it particularly difficult for ensuring effective strategic plan implementation. In such situations, consider the next option.

<u>Option 2) Appoint a lead director:</u> Given how time consuming it is to serve as board chair, especially of a complicated organization (e.g., hospital, university), consider empowering another volunteer director to fulfill some of the responsibilities expected of a board chair, especially relating to strategic plan implementation.

A lead director can assist the chair, either because of the chair's time constraints or because the chair has little management or board experience (e.g., musician chairing a social services board). It isn't unusual for a board chair to discover the duties are more time consuming than anticipated. Sometimes a chair muddles along and even the most tactful CEO is hesitant to address the gap in expected performance.

At first glance, adding a lead director to the structure of a nonprofit board seems to formalize a new position in a way that could impede the relationship between the chair, vice chair, CEO and other board members. The lead director should be viewed as just the opposite, as the for-profit world has demonstrated by keeping the focus on strategy and helping the board chair resolve difficult situations. The lead director can help the CEO work more effectively and efficiently with board committees, especially in driving the work of the strategic planning groups and assessing outcomes and impacts. What's more, the lead director can be an additional consultant or mentor to the CEO, especially when the board chair is unavailable. Because the lead director would help the board operate better, this move could also go far in building morale within the nonprofit.

Maintaining board focus on the plan

Every board meeting agenda will need to have time for updates of outcomes and impacts of the plan, and this topic should be given priority on agendas. Board retreats are also frequently used to get all groups together, including many not intimately involved with the overall work of the strategic planning committee. The author recently observed one retreat that brought the board, management and staff together to develop a significant consensus about the need to "reinvent" the nonprofit. It's recommended that a similar small-scale retreat needs to take place about six months after plan adoption to help keep board focus on strategy.

Updating the full plan

The entire strategic plan should be reviewed and updated every three to five years. Every nonprofit should be honest about answering this question: "Who would miss our organization if we ceased to exist?" Broad consideration of the responses and subsequent investigation can lead to open discussions to consider opportunities for strategic renewal. Be aware, however, that sometimes such discussions can bring about internal board conflict as those tied to the legacy of the organization strive to use every opportunity to "remember how great we've been" or "the need to retain our family atmosphere."

Takeaway

Strategic plans are of value and implementation is robust only if the nonprofit board, on a consistent basis, carefully overviews implementation and if visionary directors and managers take ownership. Plus the CEO and COO (chief operating officer) need to buy in fully, or needed change won't happen.

CHAPTER 15

THE MERGER OF TWO NONPROFITS:
WHAT IT TAKES TO SUCCEED

B oards may decide to seek a merger with a compatible organization in order to address declining prospects, eliminate service overlaps, fill gaps in service portfolios, achieve greater overall impact, or for other reasons. But whether merging (or attempting to do so) will create synergy for a nonprofit or put it on a collision course depends on how board members, in partnership with management, tackle this critical job.

Let's begin with a real-world story that can help provide a basic outline about what's needed for a merger to succeed. Following the field story, key issues that need to be addressed in the merger of two equal partners planning to form a new organization, are listed.

Field Story: Told from a 17-Year Perspective

The author looks back from the vantage point of 2016 on a merger that occurred more than 17 years ago, when Family Service America (established 1911) merged with the National Association of Homes and Services to Children (established 1973) to form the Alliance for Children & Families. Known today as the Alliance for Strong Families and Communities, it represents 450 member organizations in the U.S. and Canada that deliver a wide range of human services to people in great need. Or as someone once put it, "To run a finger down the membership roll of the Alliance is in many ways to trace the backbone of the social safety net in this country."[9]

The author chaired Family Service America's investigating committee for the merger process. Following the merger in October 1998 he served as co-chair of the Alliance board during its two-year transition period. FAQs below are the author's responses to questions he's frequently received based on first-hand experience.

Frequently Asked Questions

Q. *What was the reality the two nonprofits faced prior to the merger?*

A. Both organizations had declining membership numbers and knew they couldn't financially survive on their own. Prior to their talks, each nonprofit had sought merger partners elsewhere without success.

Q. *What was the focus of their initial merger discussions?*
A. Discussions focused on mission, vision and values, and these were deemed to be highly compatible. Both groups recognized their board compositions were very different. One board was largely composed of volunteer directors, who had director experiences with local family agencies. The other was largely composed of operating CEOs of homes, including, at the time, very large and well known ones like Boys Town.

Q. *What professional advice did the nonprofits get?*
A. Both groups separately sought legal and accounting counsel as needed. For example, the boards, per legal advice, agreed what actions would need to be taken if the merger dissolved within two years. In addition, the groups applied for a foundation grant to cover merger costs, such as severance pay for some personnel.

Q. *What were the key issues that drove the options you explored?*
A. There were many key issues including facilities, overlaps in management duties, potential personnel terminations, and board leadership during the transition. One nonprofit had a large office facility and staff located in Milwaukee and a legislative office in Washington D.C. The other had a small combined office in Washington. The joint committee recommended which personnel

positions should be eliminated, and agreed that the new Alliance board would have co-chairs for the first two years, one from each of the merging organizations. In addition, the committee decided early on that the Alliance would be led by the nationally known president/CEO of one of the organizations (Family Service America). On these and other issues that arose, the two groups were able to make compromises without encountering a significant "deal breaker."

Q. *Could you draw on the merger experience and expertise of board members?*

A. No board member from either organization had prior merger experience, but the joint merger committee was able to move through the merger process relatively smoothly.

Q. *When did you communicate the decision to merge to stakeholders?*

A. Some major funders were quietly notified as discussions were taking place, largely because the organizations needed to seek support to cover merger costs. The merger was announced publicly once both boards had approved it. The announcement made clear it was a joining of equals, not an acquisition by the larger nonprofit. Soon after the announcement, however, the executive director of the other organization resigned. As a result, that nonprofit's board employed an interim executive director until merging operations could be completed.

Q. *How smoothly did actual implementation go?*

A. The first six to nine months the merger worked well. No one, however, seemed to recognize the new organization was in a "honeymoon period." A former director on one board who became an Alliance director, and who also served as president/CEO of a local organization, later summarized the major cultural problem the Alliance encountered.

> *"Agency executives like me are used to running the show and having the leadership. As executive directors, it is something we fight for all the time with our own boards — we don't want them (the boards) to micromanage us. But as board members in the Alliance situation, there was a sense of 'who is in charge here?' We finally (realized) we have to be able to give the (CEO of the new Alliance) the space to run things."*

About a decade after the merger became effective, the Alliance's first President and CEO, the late Peter Goldberg, made this comment.

> *"The first three years of merger implementation were very tough. Anytime you do change, everybody feels threatened. The question becomes, 'Can you focus on what you are going to gain in the future, as opposed to what you're going to lose from the past?' At a*

certain point, the board and leadership real-ized that fighting for the past was destructive, and we needed to orient to the future. The al-ternative for both organizations was to take a slow respectable ride to oblivion. I have never liked that destination."

Issues to Address for "Equal" Partners Merging Into a New Organization

Assuming both organizations have merger committees that meet frequently over an extend-ed time period, the following are initial issues that need review.

a) Are the mission, vision and values of both organizations the same or sufficient-ly similar?

b) Are there any financial issues that might cloud negotiations?

c) Do the two merger committees work well together and view each other positively as potential colleagues?

d) Are both groups willing to invest the board time and financial resources to bring about a melding of the two groups?

e) Are there any factions in either of the two organizations that emotionally might be opposed to the merger?

f) What, at this early stage, might be some barriers (i.e., deal breakers) to the merger?

g) What needs to be done to move the merger process forward and to develop an implementation plan, if both boards agree to the merger?

h) How will the impact of the merger be determined and at what intervals will it be measured?

i) In the event that either or both organizations are dissatisfied with the merger, what specific details need to be in a "prenuptial" breakup agreement?

j) How will the CEO of the merged organization be determined amicably?

k) How can morale at both organizations be maintained at positive levels during merger discussions? What incentives need to be developed for those who will most likely need new jobs (e.g., a chief financial officer)?

The Devil is in the Details — Are the Following "Deal Breakers?"

- How can consensus be achieved among the various stakeholders who might be impacted by the merger (e.g., members, clients, community leaders, managers, staff, funders, vendors)?
- Where will the new nonprofit be physically located, and what are the real estate implications?

- How will decisions about layoffs and new reporting arrangements be made?
- How will the new board be constituted? Will a larger board be necessary, and if not, what will be the plan for paring down the size of the new board?
- What legal counsel will be needed, and at what cost?
- Will foundation support be needed to establish the merger, and if so how will support be secured?
- What systems or interpersonal relationships are necessary to avoid "surprises" before or after the merger?

Takeaway

Every merger will leave its own footprint. Yet blending two cultures into one new one isn't a simple task. Bumps in the road will be apparent, usually starting about six months after the merger, and continuing for several years. Although the mission, vision and values of the two nonprofits that merge may have been identical, cultural differences will definitely arise. These can be resolved — given time, persistence, CEO commitment, and board leadership.

OTHER HELPFUL GUIDELINES

CHAPTER 16

How to Use Board Members' Time Wisely

Highly qualified board candidates often turn down positions on nonprofit boards by saying "I'm too busy right now." While that may very well be the case, such a response might also be a polite way of saying, "When you say the word 'nonprofit' I think of slow processes, board agendas loaded with minutiae, presentations longer than they need to be, and unfocused discussions." You can change such perceptions if your nonprofit can deliver on the following.

- Board meetings begin and end on time, and there's a quorum present the entire time.
- Directors receive both the meeting agenda and information "binders" one week prior to the board meeting.

- Minutes are available within a week of the meeting, allowing anyone who missed the session to stay up to date.
- When a director is traveling and can participate in the meeting by conference call, the organization has the capability to enable participation by phone.
- There's a time limit allotted when there is a staff report, and the report is prepared well in advance, with the CEO working ahead of time with the presenter.
- The board chair quickly refocuses discussions that get off track.
- The maximum number of slides in a PowerPoint presentation is 10.
- Policy and strategic topics (not day-to-day operations) are the board's focus.
- Board committee work is aligned with directors' interests and backgrounds, and committee chairs understand directors' time constraints.
- The board chair and/or CEO check-in periodically with directors to ensure their actual experience matches the above guidelines.

CHAPTER 17

WHEN AND HOW TO UTILIZE
AN ADVISORY BOARD

The two reasons for having an advisory board are a) to seek advice and expertise regarding a current major project or issue and b) to provide ongoing support and guidance to the CEO. The author has found that for some nonprofits the counsel provided by a group of unaffiliated members of the community or industry can complement the existing board, helping to deliver services or products to clients with greater effect.

Advisory boards have no legal responsibilities, and no authority to require the elected board or staff members to act on their advice. However, when this board's advice is not followed, the CEO has a professional responsibility to show how the suggestions were seriously considered and to carefully report on what transpired in the decision process. Too many valuable advisory board members become disillusioned with serving in such a capacity when this step is omitted.

- *Who Could Be Asked to Serve?*
  a) People who bring unique knowledge and skills to areas in which the board and/or staff need outside viewpoints.
  b) Termed-out directors who maintain interest in the nonprofit. Recognize that members of the advisory board should be at similar executive levels in their professional fields.
  c) Leaders in the community who have broad strategic backgrounds that can be readily useful, even if their day-to-day experiences are far afield from the nonprofit's work.

- *What Should Be Conveyed in "the Ask?"*
  Rationale for the group's existence, scope of work, and frequency of meetings (three or four a year is optimal), and preparation time expected, which should be minimal.

  Also, why the person is being asked to participate and what he or she might gain in return.

- *What Does a Successful Process Look Like?*
  ○ A member of the advisory board is designated chairperson to facilitate meeting discussions.
  ○ Agendas cover only policy or strategy topics.
  ○ Meetings are scheduled well in advance.

- ○ Detailed presentations by the CEO are avoided, and the focus is on capitalizing on the abilities of the participants.
- ○ The location of meetings has a physical environment that is high quality.
- ○ Between meetings the CEO keeps important information flowing, and details where suggestions have been helpful.
- ○ The CEO and advisory board chair do post-meeting critiques to evaluate impact.
- ○ The CEO and advisory chair recognize when the group has delivered its advice and counsel and has served its usefulness.

CHAPTER 18

E ven though hiring and promotion decisions fall under the purview of the CEO, every nonprofit board has a responsibility to overview the talent bank for key staff positions below the CEO level. Succession should be an annual discussion topic on the board's agenda. To keep a clear focus, even when change isn't imminent, the board needs to have some interpersonal contact with key staff. This allows the board to be in a position to make a rapid decision for an interim CEO, if ever needed. Observing a staff person making an occasional management presentation just isn't sufficient to make judgments about the individual's leadership potential.

At the very least, when a new CEO is appointed, the board needs to determine who on staff has the necessary qualities to be an interim CEO, if needed. If there is no one, the board needs to qualify capable outsiders who can step in.

Talent development and succession planning need to be developed as a director responsibility and strategic leadership skill. This takes board time and energy but the organization can pay dearly at a transition period for a CEO if this responsibility is neglected for years.

CHAPTER 19

UNDERSTAND HOW MILLENNIALS
IMPACT NONPROFITS

By the year 2020 millennials will comprise more than one of three adult Americans. It is estimated that by 2025 they will make up as much as 75% of the workforce.[10] Although millennials working requirements and values may puzzle older board cohorts, as millennials begin to populate boards their dedication to nonprofits' missions will likely be outstanding.

Yet for some years to come, most board members can expect to have their most frequent contact with their nonprofit's millennials while working with staff on task forces and special projects. Directors need to be aware that the millennial generation's work styles are requiring changes within the nonprofit. Key things to know:

Work-life balance — Millennials don't have a rigid demarcation between work and personal life. Home, libraries and coffee houses are often seen as desirable places to be productive. They also expect substantially more personal accommodations (e.g., scheduling adjustments for family responsibilities). Making these adjustments will require a nonprofit board to review human resource policies, since most nonprofits do not have much "bench strength" in terms of personnel to easily make these accommodations.

Flexible work spaces — If more staff use laptops, which is typical of millennials, and if the nonprofit has a cloud-based IT system, the nonprofit will require less fixed-based computer equipment and less fixed office space.

Food — having free food may make sense. The questions to answer are: do the benefits of having the staff together for another hour a day, discussing problems and generating team-building efforts outweigh the costs, and does doing so offer opportunities for staff to informally interact with senior managers? Costs and sources of revenue to cover them would have to be addressed by nonprofits considering such a move.

Physical facilities — If possible, some thought should be given to office ambiance. A casual attire workplace has already taken hold nationally. Both are progressive moves designed to meet the value systems of the millennial generation. In addition, since some millennials are prone to work non-stop hours to complete a project, consideration needs to be given to providing space for relaxation.

REFERENCES

1   Urban Institute (2015) "The Nonprofit Sector in Brief: Public Charities, Giving & Volunteering," October

2   BoardSource (2015) *Leading With Intent—A National Index of Nonprofit Board Practices*, Washington, DC, January

3   Ibid,

4   Kamla D. Harris (2008) "The New 990 and It's Relationship to California Law," Office of the Attorney General, State of California, Department of Justice

5   BoardSource (2015) *Leading With Intent—A National Index of Nonprofit Board Practices*, Washington, DC, January

6   Peter Murray & Steve Ma (2015) The Promise of Lean Experimentation, *Stanford Social Innovation Review,* Summer

7   http://www.dwt.com/Directors-of-Nonprofit-Held-Financially-Liable-for-Relying-on-Incompetent-Officers-and-Lack-of-Oversight-03-06-2015/

8   http://www.bridgespan.org/Publications-and-Tools/Nonprofit-Boards/Resources-for-Board-Members/Nonprofit-Boards-Role-in-Onboarding-a-New-CEO.aspx#.VtCR_RjLMz4

9   http://www.bridgespan.org/Blogs/Cliff-Notes-Government-Nonprofits-and-Philanthropy/August-2011/Remembering-Peter-Goldberg.aspx

10 http://www.brookings.edu/research/papers/2014/05/millenials-upend-wall-street-corporate-america-winograd-hais

INDEX

About the Author

E ugene H. Fram, Ed.D., is an expert in nonprofit governance, a business consultant and an award-winning emeritus professor of the Saunders College of Business at Rochester Institute of Technology (RIT). He is also the author of six other books and more than 125 published articles, and has been widely quoted by national media on topics ranging from marketing to business to high performance nonprofits. His blog on nonprofit governance has 2000 followers.

He is a past recipient of RIT's highest award for outstanding teaching and one of a very select group awarded the Presidential Medallion, given to those making exceptionally significant contributions to the university. In 2012, a former student anonymously contributed $3 million to endow an RIT Chair in Critical Thinking in his name, an honor Dr. Fram describes as "a professor's dream come true!"

Over his distinguished career he has served on 12 nonprofit boards overseeing diverse community, national and professional organizations, and also has served on five for-profit boards. His particular passion is helping nonprofit boards perform at high levels as more is expected of these boards today than most people realize. He credits his frequent collaborator, writer/editor Vicki Brown, for exceptional creativity in turning the lessons he's learned into this highly valuable guidebook.

Eugene Fram lives in Los Altos, California. Vicki Brown resides in Rochester, New York.

Another Book for Nonprofit Boards by the Author

Policy vs. Paper Clips: How Using the Corporate Model Makes a Nonprofit Board More Efficient & Effective was written by Eugene Fram with Vicki Brown, who has extensive career experience with nonprofits as writer, editor, employee, board chair and director. The book, now in its third edition, has been updated and expanded. It is being used by many nonprofits to make their governance structure stronger and, in turn, their boards more productive. It addresses using the organizational format called the Corporate Model. The model was first introduced by Dr. Fram in 1975 and has now been tried and adopted, the author estimates, by thousands of boards across the U.S.

At its core the book is about separating operational and policy issues, which sounds simple, but isn't. It requires a fundamental change in a nonprofit's culture that promotes new relationships and communication styles from the top to the bottom rung of an organization. It's a serious book about a serious topic, but written in a highly readable, engaging style.

Contacts:
Eugene H. Fram: frameugene@gmail.com
650-209-5724 (PT)

Vicki Brown: vickibrown05@gmail.com

POLICY

vs. *paper clips*

EUGENE H. FRAM
WITH VICKI BROWN

3rd Edition

updated and expanded

how using the corporate model makes a nonprofit board more efficient & effective

Available at Amazon — http://amzn.to/eu7nQl

66627124R00078

Made in the USA
Charleston, SC
24 January 2017